From the Watercolor Garden: Poems of Life and Love

Ty Gardner

Copyright © 2020 by Ty Gardner

Cover art copyright © 2020 by Shelly Gardner

All rights reserved. No part of this publication may be reproduced, stored in a retrieval system, or transmitted in any form or by any means, electronic, mechanical, photocopying, recording, or otherwise without written permission of the copyright owner except for the use of quotations in a book review.

For more information, address: gardnty@gmail.com

ISBN: 9798577186821

When the winds of poetry are at your back,
fly high on wings of words.

Table of Contents

The Nexus That Connects Us	12
Little Things Adorned	13
A Tale of Fire	14
Inroads to Idling	15
Lines and Steady Hands	16
Conspiring Hearts	17
A Bard Heart's Blight	18
Stories From the Balconies	19
High Seas Remorse	20
The Steward's Fall	21
Silence in Psalm-hands	22
What Luck?	23
May You Everything	24
Heart Tempo Love Song	25
A Telling of Brevity	26
We'll Shout on High	27
Watchful Eyes of Weeping Willows	28
Overtones and Parables	29
Boudoir Biology	30
Epicurean Crossroads	31
Crush	32
Love, Electric	33
Dream Angel's Opus	34

Central Texas Rhythm	35
Sunshine Smile	36
Caged-heart Companions	37
From the Watercolor Garden	38
Good Tidings Bird	39
Beneath the Sway and Bramble	40
On Days Like This	41
Sanguine Smiles and Dallied-love	42
Folds of Velveteen	43
These Things I Give	44
The Lady, Gretel	45
Moon Song Matrimony	46
Mindful Truths	47
The Fruits of Love	48
Island Eyes and Paradise	49
Celestine	50
Father's Promise	51
The Cosmic Mezzanine	52
Of Silken Tears	53
Ink Waves On Paper Oceans	54
Love in Layers	55
A Passage to Passion	56
Hues of Amaranth	57

Orion-smile Skies	58
Of Ambry and Absence	59
Heart Cloud Fancies	60
Beyond, Beyond	61
Ode to a Smile	62
A Bond in Words	63
Hay-scatter Eternity	64
Moonless Musing	65
To Love We Spoke	66
Plot Hole Love	67
A Prayer in Erns't	68
Ephemeral Mortality	69
Picasso Poetess	70
Hindsight Homily	71
Alas, These Shearing Hands	72
Mourning Hearts	73
Ember Ends in Midnight Moons	74
The Shepherding	75
Favor of the Waxing Moon	76
Backseat Intrigue	77
Delivered	78
To Dance, I Plead	79
In Wistful Woods	80

Down Starlit Streets	81
In Bitter Winter Winds	82
Asides and Courtships	83
Window Dust Abandon	84
Tales of How We Love	85
Bane of Storied-hearts	86
A Dare to Dream	87
A Sentiment for Totem Hearts	88
Fine Lines and Finger-feet	89
The Longing Call	90
Remember Me, Remembering You	91
Huntress Dawn	92
The Way We Moved	93
Summer's Timekeepers	94
Traces of the Way We Covet	95
Island Queen	96
All Things You	97
Shoebox Memory Romance	98
Galway Seas and Busking	99
Shenandoah Sweethearts	100
Cool Grass Contemplations	101
Skyline Tributes	102
A Love Song Poem	103

Languor of Love	104
In Tones of Sepia	105
Love Like Whiskey	106
Prism People	107
Coalescence Like Stars	108
Sweetgrass Pleasantries	109
Melodies in Reverie	110
Little Whispers, Big Secrets	111
Midnight Youth	112
Dandelion Daydream	113
Acknowledgments	115
About the Author	117

The Nexus That Connects Us

Cinnabar and Sego,
        you place a tacked thumb to mine
and press the mysteries of your pedigree through
pattern, print, and plasm;
        past layers bodhi lush
and push,
        pulling,
languishing to better know your bawdy language,
        bodies languid,
burning up the nexus that connects us.

Little Things Adorned

Sterling and jade, although amethyst by birthright,
hers are hands adored of little things adorned—poppy tops twirled in the tips
of her fingers and the touch of breeze-dried linen.

She's beautiful with no place to go
but doesn't hold it against me; selfless like a poem.

A Tale of Fire

It's fire,

    this heat-hot thing I have for you;

        bubble brewing talk of sex and mess,

            of trips to lost and all the rest, it's fire.

That fire that sutures every stitch of bond between the peaks that glow,

and the night sky's kiss, it's fire.

Inroads to Idling

Ocean dawn,

we swirl in streams and currents—courses and channels of least resistance.

    Inroads
           and
                outlets,

we bend and stray idly from those rhythms.

And when our time is over, barren creek bed rubble;

rolled round and sun-bleached like revenant remnants of rivers old.

Lines and Steady Hands

Slighted fingers tremble at the temptation of touching you.
Such considerations dare not be made in haste.

There are lines and strokes canyon-deep that are breathtaking to behold;
aesthetic brilliance of the Master that should be regarded as such.

Steady my hand, I pray.

Conspiring Hearts

I push you down to pull me in;
your passion-waves bid sink or swim.

To paint your portrait pleasure-red,
the masterstroke, a brush needs thread.

And to the crest of peaks desired,
a journey bourn of hearts conspired.

The planted stem crowned height to power,
his queen, in florets, shall petal flower.

A Bard Heart's Blight

No lines between us that can't be crossed;

    words that can't be said or thought.

Nothing but borders and boundaries

    between<>us—open space and states to drive us insane.

But bard hearts endure betweens,

    the missing pains and wanting things.

Stories From the Balconies

We live them in the sweat of cola-frosted glass,

the streaked reflections of simpler times.

Hark the call of them when they wet your aging hand and shout the

splashed-creek stories of your youth from the balcony

of the world that they might hear your words in the heavens.

High Seas Remorse

Of shipwrecked hands, we cast away.
On bible verse smote skies of gray.

Susurrus winds to sing our tale,
the chiming of the love-toll bell.

A quilt of love notes never sent,
our sails did mast the forged regret.

The Steward's Fall

A steward,

    nude,

and his ribbed companion,

    did set upon a branched-fruit,

supple in splendor and shimmering charm.

        Behest by serpentine schemes,

    they did receive and spoke at length of things not known before.

    And at once, the skies did weep a steady stream eternal.

Silence in Psalm-hands

Hosanna-speak my name no more;
your closed-eyes-to-blue-sky hallelujahs I beg, adjourn.

A silence to psalm-hand praises and mountain high rejoicing, I ask.
Know strength in humanity by the coos' of babes and softening grip
of parting loved ones.

In simple things, I beg.

What Luck?

What luck is this, to know your love?

To think nothing of hims, hers, theys,

and thems—stepping stone staircases to a state of mind I can stand behind.

What luck is this, to feel a heartbeat skip a thousand miles away and think

                                                        nothing of distance?

What luck...

May You Everything

May you dance reckless the guilty pleasures of your heart.

Know the wisdom of stars while walking through foreign lands.

Steal a kiss from a stranger and punch clocks outside of work.

May you be alive in your life.

Heart Tempo Love Song

The flutter-thump pounding of racing hearts

                is the tempo I want to write you love songs.

A Telling of Brevity

Today I knew the scents of autumn air in the finity of marshes wild.

    Creatures of spring,
        and winters vast,

converged on the muddy banks where cattail cotton

festered and bosomed aloft to spread their stories far and wide.

There was a telling of brevity, but I lingered.

We'll Shout on High

Dwell not in follied-larks of old—stepping stones o'er river tides;

(hidden paths to yous untold.)

Come, and speak of love with me.
It's strength and how it sets you free.

On mountain high, we'll shout of love.
To lakes and valleys far below, to stars and heaven far above.

Watchful Eyes of Weeping Willows

Stings and smarts to think you in dreams,

                                          the only place we've ever met,

bare-backed in the looming of beaming moonlight,

                              bathing in it, basking in bodies undulating,

breathing, breathless, breaking skin
and building bonds beneath the watchful eye of a willow, weeping.

Overtones and Parables

Parables in parallels; equinox tales of smiles wide as ocean tides,
and days-long nights on dreamscape dance floors.

See me there, celestial goddess, and giggle-kiss in crushed velvet surplice.

Overtones of "Clair de Lune" to play us into the mythos of the universe.

Boudoir Biology

That one time,

when it was all mess and sex and countertop encounters of the rough kind—
archeological stuff when we would dig into each other's bad habits and break
the monotony with boudoir biology.

When it was peach tree paradise without pity, flavored,

that one time.

Epicurean Crossroads

Awhile longer, that I might memorize your everything;

the straightaways before the bends and curves
that read like road maps to the places I love most,
the pit stops to pluck your fruit and drip sweet the juices of your bounty.

Awhile longer that I might bask and breathe your scent.

Crush

There's a disheartening of hardened
hearts who've only met in dreams,
who've never held their lover's gaze
'neath looming beams of midnight's moon,
never known the positive power of negative
hands on crushed napes, bruising the bronchi,
begging for breath, bracing for sweet relief.

Love, Electric

A wondrous thing to be loved and in love.
A curious magic sent down from above.

It's the shimmer-reflection of an eved-sun glow'n wave.
The blood rush sensation in kisses, we crave.

So invite love electric; a shock wave bliss-jolt.
Let it firework charm you, a lightning love bolt.

Dream Angel's Opus

A dream exchange, in prudence theme, an Angel did confer.

To these he spoke, I hear them now, of life rules to refer:

"believe beliefs; stand spirit-tall,

you've kingdom-heaven skies to reach still after all.

Be kind with love, the frail heart's key, in turn, rewards of bliss.

Take care to care, big dreams do dare, be not a friend remiss."

He turned again, a parting thought, his opus high note leave:

"do good when evil rears its head, and your soul shall know reprieve."

Central Texas Rhythm

Mandolin grass lullabies and banjo string wildflowers

    are the sweet sounds

of the wide-open plains of central Texas.

    And my heartbeat dips and soars

to the bend and sway of their folk-rhythm soul.

Sunshine Smile

Bastille me in those jail cell eyes;
the sentence served is worth the prize.

We're childish hearts in forts of sheets,
we chase and kiss, we're giggle-bliss,

                         a knockout love they can't defeat.

So meet me splashed of puddled-rain,
and hold me through the storm.

In darkest nights and bitter cold,
your sunshine smile will keep me warm.

Caged-heart Companions

Caged-heart companions are forever aware of the tragedy of their passion.

Bound by a love that is simply too great to be contained,
we are moved by their fate.

For some things cannot be known by way of words,
but through time and patience.

The latter being the sincerity of love.

From the Watercolor Garden

From the watercolor garden,

      poems of life and love—postcards and post-its passed between

            paramour-hands in picnicked-blanket sanctity.

Sacred things said in the savor of their lover's favor,

the space between the lines where rainstorm reveries take place and kisses

spark electric.

Good Tidings Bird

Take flight and fly, to the clouds, to the sky!
Regale bemused life's woes on high.

Speak not, sweet bird, of wax-winged things;
unfurl refrained what joy yours brings.

Of sanguine-quilted spirits soar,
good tidings one and all implore.

Beneath the Sway and Bramble

Plant this garden mind in soil strong,

    beneath the sway of

        kaleidoscoping-skies where even time

can't trespass the thorny bramble.

Burrow down shallow plots that fruited-words will bud

    and

flourish from clay and loam.

Find me there, alive and well, in planted thoughts.

On Days Like This

On days like this,

I miss the air on mountains high.

I've thoughts of swatting clustered-cloud pillow wisps and closed-eye hand-to-God-hallelujahs for the million breaths I've exhaled.

I miss the creaking branch wind chime choruses of the wild;

on days like this...

Sanguine Smiles and Dallied-love

Goodnight, sweet moon.

Sovereign queen of hallowed filigree.

Aloft to the twinkle-eyed gaze of the empyrean expanse,

a gossamer of sanguine smiles and dallied-love daydreams.

Folds of Velveteen

Sink me in your velveteen, and fold me in your plush.

I long for feathered tufts of crimson root,
seeped in honey'd-heather to nourish and give me strength.

To kiss collisions of astral fields and know my final form:

nothing and everything at once—pure, loving, energy.

These Things I Give

To the stars, I give my eyes,
                                that they may shine eternal.

My soul to the sun that my fiery passion
                                will warm the bones of generations.

To the moon, my smile,
                                that all who gaze upon her know no tears.

These gifts I leave for the world,
                                that they might know my heart.

The Lady, Gretel

Candy sweet with Hansel eyes, I love her Gretel bravery.
She stands tall when they shut her out, when monsters rapt her savory.
The flaming sword in darkest wood, a swelter shadows dread.
The world's no frosted ginger-house, and she's come to bake their bread.

Moon Song Matrimony

As I remember her:

    the
        September
                sun setting in the west;

adorned with grace and silhouetted-roses white,
crimson-cheeked and nervous,

she glided gently into the fold of love
and comfort—welcome arms, true and steady.

The evening moon whistled a starlight serenade to celebrate her smile.

Mindful Truths

Huddle close your futures sired,
heads to breast with burden eyes,
and smile-sigh your response to pied-sky notions,
mindful of their delicate nature.

Shelter notions of hard truths and the cruel joke of death despite
our best efforts to live. Huddle them close and smile.

The Fruits of Love

Plant me in your garden dear,
and let my love seed grow.

In time our fruit you'll come to bear,
a gift I long to know.

Yes, plant me in your garden dear,
that our essence might live on.

My heart knows joy that pieces stay,
long after we are gone.

Island Eyes and Paradise

Of love, my dear, a simple thought:

to haven shores, let's chart a course; of spells, we'll craft our ships.

Your island eyes, a paradise, there's magic in your lips.

Celestine

Celestine, she knows his heart. Knows him backward, end to start.

Neverminds his wandering eyes, forgive/forgets his childish lies.

Celestine, she knows his mind. Knows the place he's now confined.

Sees his struggle reminiscing; looking for the pieces missing.

Hears his thoughts when no one's listening.

Celestine, she knows his heart.

Father's Promise

In faith,

an outstretched hand to mine—contact;
a fusion of minds and memories and lives yet to be lived.

And beneath a blanket-bundling of 'coos,
a father's wetted-eye whispered-promise
of all the magic this world has to offer.

The Cosmic Mezzanine

Afoot the cosmic mezzanine,
                        providence beheld the rupture in your rapture.

The grandeur of which penetrated the expansive sable,
                        allowing the bespecklement of heavens plight

to favor the farthest reaches of the darkest corners.

                        Celestial, yours is embodiment divine.

Of Silken Tears

There's something silk, and lotion-smooth about the way you cry.

How it seeps atom-deep into the soul and vibrates like ocean sand earthquakes.

Something torrential, and cleansing, about the way you cry that pours
and washes over me;
                resplendent anew.

Ink Waves On Paper Oceans

I could no longer stand the thought of being needed in your abstract.
What use is a flower without its bloom after all?

So I rose-petalled my way across   waves on paper oceans to write all of
                              ink   y

                                                                                    o

                                                                                    u

                                                                                    r

                                                                                    w

                                                                                    r

                                                                                    o

                                                                                    n

                                                                                    g

                                                                                    s.

Love in Layers

Only in layers can it be strengthened.

Slowly, and with patience to let it settle,
does it allow itself to receive kindness.

It is then that we can sand and smooth its rough edges and apply our colors.

And if we puncture it,
we can repeat the process carefully and heal it,
removing all traces of damage.

The walls of love, our greatest labor.

A Passage to Passion

Press them in, pursed lips to mine—promises of passage to passion.

But are we more than just pursuits in wild abandon?

Than wanton whims in blushed-cheeks and loose hair brush back flirtations?

What of love and Neruda's call to the "Flowery One?"

Can we live forever in poetry?

Hues of Amaranth

Long for the roads that bridle passioned-reds of lady amaranth,
I shelled my mortal body long ago.

To wander free from purpose and divine contraction,
to indulge the follies of curtained-hearts exquisite and remember them,

regal as morning hues unperturbed by ashen-sky.

Orion-smile Skies

Immured of raging sea protestations,
        we braced ourselves in breaking-bow strength.

To the iron will of Orion-smile skies, we cast our gaze,
        and in the trumpeting sounds of the earthborn warrior,

we found the courage to stay our spirits and sail on;
        aloft to constellations uncharted.

Of Ambry and Absence

And so a time will come,

faultless and fair-skinned in that moment you rooted her

    deep
        in the ambry of seascaped-memoirs,

to embrace necessity in quietude.

To know yourself hearted in the melody of rafter beams that swell and sob in her absence;

because all things must grieve.

Heart Cloud Fancies

Eyes closed,

                         my face to the sun,

I cast a string of love lines into blue sky oceans

           hoping to catch the fancy of wandering heart clouds.

Beyond, Beyond

Hats off to the horizon, that place beyond, Beyond—a crossroads to dreamscapes and adventures in stick sword shenanigans.

Hats off to living our story and keeping a weather eye to the west; weary and wanting of exploits that abide our restless spirits.

Ode to a Smile

Flash me wonky crowned-gum pearls, I love that heart-lined smile.

There's waves at sunset in your grin, come hold my hand there for a while.

So to the simper-beam that sits the width of dimpled stride,

a banjo bluegrass-fusioned toast to praise your sainted visage pride.

A Bond in Words

Our bond is words and love for love—paragraph exchanges in
sentenced-fragments of poetic passion.

A bond in reasonless rhyme,
and no rhymes to reason with
rules that ruin and run rampant with regrets.

Grace adorned our bond that binds a love for love.

Hay-scatter Eternity

We're nothing more than ghosts, my dear, and simply cannot love.

    Not truly.

For ours is the moted-particles of a cracked barn door summer's eve sunlight.

    A silhouette's pirouette of kicked up hay-scatter and nothing more.

The length of eternity is definable of it.

Moonless Musing

On moonless nights, when the stars have the sky to themselves,

I lay in meadows where silence muses peacefully,

and I watch her naked form in the sky sway to a rhythm known only to the universe.

To Love We Spoke

Amid the hollow eyes of dust-framed ancestry, we spoke:
tales of dustbowl depression and flat cap first-time fancies.

Of black-strapped boots to ground in far off lands—
glory days of blood and battle.

But to love, we spoke the most.
The special kind to help you home.

Plot Hole Love

Push me in your subplot holes, we need to work things out.

Our story arc's bamboozle-browed, we curve in lines of tout.

So let them chirp in daybreak hours, the shadow cricket bands,

our psalms of salt and pillered-love; our gospel ghosting hands.

A Prayer in Erns't

I prayed in erns't to God today.
Prayed your pain to take away.

Cried a thunder-rain to come, and wash away the hate of death.
Blister-bruised my fists in dirt with hopeful alms of final breath.

I prayed in erns't to lose a friend,
the words were sharp and cut to say.

The words I prayed in erns't to God,
to take away your pain today.

Ephemeral Mortality

At length, upon the ephemeral terrace of mortality, I stood.

The drama of brassed-steel skies resounding a thundering rendition of "Moonlight Sonata" o'erhead as I reflected a cavalcade of triumphs and defeats.

Of that waning term,

I closed my eyes.

                        Ascension come to pass.

Picasso Poetess

Cola lips, sugar sweet and cherry red,

let's talk with tongues and have a chat about paradise in palpitations of pulsing hearts.

You're sodalicious when you speak of quilted-souls pieced and placed with patchwork precision—a painter with your poetry,
                                                muse me as you will.

Hindsight Homily

        A message now to fledgling ears of clipped-wing love not meant to fly:
                              the hours spent on wasted tears,

in time you'll find hurt less to cry.

                Your heart's a crucible of melted, molten passions pooled.

Let not the fumes of fires dimmed, harden-pack, and leave you cooled.

Alas, These Shearing Hands

What treasures waning moons impart to the bold;
        trinkets in pieces of fleeting love.

Flowers bloom and receive in her luminescence,
        and one need only extend a simple courtesy to know the
        the splendor of their petals.

But alas, these shearing hands are artists of drawing last breaths,
        and I dare not reach for them.

Mourning Hearts

I think I'll mourn a heart today.

I held it once, in cupped-hands, but baby birds are wanton to

        spread their wings and fly away.

Try as I might to hold it back in riddles and rhymes,

        through stanzas of time, baby birds are wanton to away;

I think I'll mourn a heart today.

Ember Ends in Midnight Moons

With crows a-flight in sprawling green,
we walked in Douglas fir and spoke of our favorite things:

        -of fishing pull tugs and purple heart patrons.
      -of cars deserted to time and dust in flaxen fields.

To front porch swings and ember ends
      of cigarettes in midnight moonlight, we spoke.

The Shepherding

Teach me to speak "I-need-yous" in the small hours of bated breathing.

Yours is the shepherding staff alight these plains of solitude,

    and I beg one last plight of companionship.

A wetted-glass gaze now the crystalline display of our life together;

    what smiles they'll see there.

Favor of the Waxing Moon

What moon is this
that waxes luminous the tender smiles of star-heart lovers?

To live
and shine among them is to know the favor of the universe.

Backseat Intrigue

Fall-fogged windows crystallize; backseat lover's paradise.

I was tremble-hands in foreign lands, you were untold future crystal eyes.

But where you've been, and where you are now, are scattered wind whispers that push the rippled time past between us further.

Delivered

Will you know the voice
that speaks and the hands that reach,
in the glaze of glass eyes and shallow lungs?

Will you know to follow
and uproot your soul of its
earthen restraints when the voice that speaks
and the hands that reach do come to speak and reach?

To Dance, I Plead

I hope you dance, my dearest friend,
where daylight's dusk meets its nightfall lover,
entwined of eager evening embrace.

                        Where wild things run free,
                  sticky sweat in sedimentary dust.

In sketchbook shadings of serendipity, I hope you dance, my dearest friend.

In Wistful Woods

In wistful woods I cared to dance.
Encouraged of its woeful silence I leapt, legs asunder.
                      Visage-rage, I welcomed thunder.

But those were moons of youth,
and the heralding sallow-song of death is upon me now.
              Those wistful woods again I soon shall dance.

Down Starlit Streets

Midnight black,
        in street less lights,
we're moon song slow dance eyes; shadows deep,

I love the layers buried in your window soul.
        Midnight black, down starlit streets we dance,
shadows deep where moons serenade our window souls.

Inertia love is effortless.

In Bitter Winter Winds

I learned the heft of death in the
whisper-whimper sobs of bitter winter winds.

Felt it in the painful, slow gait of a boy, my kin,
cradling the frozen framework of his fallen friend.

I Knew apathy then as I beheld the hardening of that fawning
child's tender heart in quiet mourning.

The heft of death, in the steady fading of my brother's love;
fading steadily as we lay a friend to rest in bitter winter winds.

Asides and Courtships

I'm taking time for taking time today.
    For cultivating love in the cumulostratosphere—painted tufts of heart-shaped clouds in beryl blue-skied oceans.

For temperament in tongue-tied typing,
I'm making time for making time.

For unspoken disclosure, asides in coffee house courtships,

I'm taking time.

Window Dust Abandon

Against the pelter-swelter of mid-summer mists, I stood before her, waxing pastoral.

Abandoned attic window dust had long since coated the small prints of childish hands,

and the height of her had resigned in the weighted sway of weeping willow whiplash.

Of this, I wept.

Tales of How We Love

There's triumph in the tragedy of ceaseless weekend one night stands.
A wisdom, ancient, lie within; the grasp of it is in our hands.

So seek thee out the ballad-bards, and put your arrows to the sky.

Let loose a stream of colored words that tales of how we love may fly.

Bane of Storied-hearts

I've love of queens, beautiful and bold.

Thunderous with inked-quills that stain
red the parchment where they lay their storied-hearts.

I've love and cupped-hands where once the bane of tender

bruise did soften those storied-hearts,
                                          no more.

I've love of mountains now.

A Dare to Dream

I've said some things that made some sense,
and sensed some things that needed said.

Painted pictographs with words I wrote and blushed the sky a pinkish hue with every swoop of penned-ink stroke.

But passion sparked in thoughts I've seamed was all I ever dared to dream.

A Sentiment for Totem Hearts

Where you were, where I was,
the skies wept torrential—a feeble-woed sentiment to
the distance between us.

For even in leaps and bounds and worlds away,

                the story of our totem hearts was known,

and the wild blues of yonder mused in hues of gray at our longing.

Fine Lines and Finger-feet

To the soft-spoken trumpet-tuts of "La Vie en rose,"
    I followed lightly,
the curves and contours of the small of you in tender finger-feet.

Gently I walked the fine line of a
    childhood scar now faded
and nearly forgotten—highways and old roads to the best parts of you.

The Longing Call

Hungover from hiatus,

                        I ache to be drunkenly delighted of your affections.

As a man maddened by the ire of burdened-moons that long for the low baying of wayward wolves, I, too, hear the siren call of your fervor summoning me to the misted Isles of Oneiric to slumber.

Remember Me, Remembering You

A sonance lie

    in the shimmer-sparkle of stars above the rushing hum of free fall winds.

One might even know

    the cooling clap of splashed-tide waves in the cascade of a sun-warmed sand embrace.

Remember me remembering you this way in the welcoming of earthly hands.

Huntress Dawn

Midnight's dawn in wasteland dreams,
I've come 'cross her scent here before.

Scotland heir to Titian hair, skin of milken-glaze, a tinting of rose in lunar beams of apples red.

Lo, she is chambered-gun, loaded with steady aim at the heart of her prey,

and I am the hunted.

The Way We Moved

On a Westbound highway,

a-cusp the sleet-mist skied outskirts of East Wells, Nevada, air castle reveries in Fleet-Foxed melodies of ragged-wood and quiet houses reminded me of the language then.

The way we moved and our manner of dress.

I loved that version of us.

Summer's Timekeepers

Magenta splashes against an ashen silhouette of what once was, theirs is a pallet of splendor that cuts through the piercing static of charred grays.

And in the space of the post frenzy lull,

a symphony of extraordinary hues renders life anew.

For they are the keepers of time here and the

seasons rise and fall to their melody.

Traces of the Way We Covet

Traces of the way we covet in the swirl
of silky residue—atonement for loving you
washed away in the reverie of hearted-exhales.

Suffuse my hands the layers of your trepidations that
you may steady and receive me.

Island Queen

raven mane beauty

shades of umber skin magic

island queen grace

All Things You

Your voice in wind, 'cross budding meadows.
Your century soul in pine bark dust.
Your poetry hands in spattered ink.
Your galaxy eyes in a springed-summer's fall.
Your big sky heart 'neath quakie byways.
Your smile in frames of dusking glow.
These things, I think and dream of you.

Shoebox Memory Romance

Sorting and sifting,
I'm closed-eyed and drifting,
a memory shoebox of romance and loss.

These fold-creased and faded
      (now cigarette-jaded)
are black and white bygones, a hefted love-cross.

So to whiskey breath sighs,
and gentle goodbyes, it's time now I took up my post.

A breeze-swayed front porch-swing,

the sounds made when chimes sing,

I, too, am a through-passing ghost.

Galway Seas and Busking

Were it here,
in high tide dreams
of Galway seas and pub-side busking for bread and wine,

like nomads of no lands,
        partisans conceived of tumbleweed and wildflower that we'd come

together to hem the frayed seams of time in pleated-pleading,

and live life in absolute.

Shenandoah Sweethearts

Just abreast the Shenandoah,
cross-legged and cradled in sweltered-skin,
a dyad braced in lusted-delivery.

Curious hands clamber and scale the fortitude of crested-form before

descending through clefted-pass to valleys,
        fields,
and streams below.
Soft exhales are lost to impassioned waters.

Cool Grass Contemplations

I want to lie in grass with you and talk about the stars.
To wonder if they're looking back with dreams of love like ours.

I need to feel the earth pass time—eternal shades of dawn.
I long to long in idol eyes of loved ones who've moved on.

Promise note these things to me and set my spirit free;
a precipice to take my flight in leisure equanimity.

Skyline Tributes

Sail with me in skies of azure blue,

    and we'll scribble red the skylines of the world;

a tribute to love and the stories it creates.

A Love Song Poem

Steal me in your plagiareyes, and copyright my wrongs.
I'll play you chords of major love in all the first crush chorus songs.

Let's ray of sunshine light the way for birds of feather mates.
We'll fortune tell the tale of those who's hearts defied their fates.

Languor of Love

A fluttering,

paced to par a hummingbird's blinked-wing exuberance
in cheeked-teeth glee that reveals the covenant made
in confidence kept.

Harbor your anchored-languor there
with graceful heart and flowered-hair as ships adrift the casted net of
impassioned eve's glow.

In Tones of Sepia

Cemetery fields of green,
                         we walked in tones of sepia overlay.

There was no one left to remember there,
and the clouds couldn't be bothered to   cry for them anyway.

I should have kissed you then,
but my hammerhead couldn't nail down my feelings for you.

Love Like Whiskey

It's things you say what keeps me up at night.

My mind a somersault of "what ifs…" and "why nots?"

The heat of it sweats the skin like desert campfire intercourse—whiskey-warm words that melt me down to puddles and precipitation; a rain for you to splash and smile.

Prism People

I knew him then in refraction,
a medium dispersing the soft light of others into brilliant colors.

The best parts of all of us shone through him,
but there was something cursory in the way he lived.

Like rippling water,
some people just aren't meant to stay in one place.

Coalescence Like Stars

Your warmth and your grace,
        post-coital embrace,
                coalescence matched only by stars.

A universe there, unlike anywhere, no richer in splendor than ours.

Sweetgrass Pleasantries

Whisper me sweetgrass pleasantries
that I might remember your smiling face against the setting sun;
wisps of a mountain breeze playfully admiring your daisy-braided hair.

A portrait of perfection awaits.

Melodies in Reverie

Place your patch-love quilted heart, and sew it to my chest.
              I want you close in thoughts refrained;
unspoken grace your eyes behest.

And in the slow of pulled-bow hairs,
                    a fiddled-voice our song will croon.

A melody in reverie, the world in whole will know our tune.

Little Whispers, Big Secrets

A living quote once whispered to me
all manner of the esoteric;
thoughts of life and love cosmos old.

Whispered of garden paradise peaks and valleys unsurpassed in beauty,

so I quashed the quote and made it mine,
forever the words to keep me going.

Midnight Youth

Down a midnight main street of "way-back-whens,"

we set our pace to a cricket wing refrain
        and pulled pond-pooled memories of youthful ignorance to the muddy
banks of our minds—projector-flashed slideshow images
        of the way things were.

Dandelion Daydream

cupped-hands, secrets hold

a dandelion life, mine

in wind, spirits soar

Acknowledgments

To my family, friends, and amazing followers, I must express eternal gratitude. Your tireless support lifts my spirits daily and continues to give me strength and inspiration in my endeavors and writing. I truly could not chase my dreams without your love. If my words have reached you in any way, please, kindly leave a review for this book. Your time and thoughts are important to me.

About the Author

A lover of words and the impact they create, Ty Gardner is a lifelong enthusiast of all forms of poetry and has written creatively from the time he was a child.

When he's not musing and waxing poetic, Ty can be found exploring the wonderment of his newfound home in Northwest Arkansas with his wife, two children, and their handsome rescue pup, Archer.

He is the author of By Way of Words: A Micro Prose Journey Through the Elements That Mold Us, Bukowski Charm: Trash Fire Poetry to Warm the Soul, Wild Life: Musings of a Mad Poet, A Thousand Little Things: One-line Poems to Spark a Thought, Exercises in the Abstract: Poems With No Name, Sunsets Over Cityscapes: Poems for the Existential Uprising, Papercut: A Chap-style Book of Prose, and Average American: Poems On Becoming Normal. Some of his works can also be found in VSS365 Anthology: Volume One, released in September 2019.